IMAGES
of America

DETROIT'S
OLYMPIA STADIUM

D1501477

IMAGES
of America

DETROIT'S
OLYMPIA STADIUM

Robert Wimmer

ARCADIA

Published by Arcadia Publishing,
an imprint of Tempus Publishing, Inc.
3047 N. Lincoln Ave., Suite 410
Chicago, IL 60657

Printed in Great Britain.

Library of Congress Catalog Card Number: 00-108399

For all general information contact Arcadia Publishing at:
Telephone 843-853-2070
Fax 843-853-0044
E-Mail sales@arcadiapublishing.com

For customer service and orders:
Toll-Free 1-888-313-2665

Visit us on the internet at http://www.arcadiapublishing.com

This one's for Diane—
Who sat with me in so many different seats
at the Olympia

CONTENTS

Acknowledgments   6

Introduction   7

1.   The '20s   9

2.   The '30s   17

3.   The '40s   23

4.   The '50s   29

5.   The '60s and '70s   53

6.   December '79 and the '80s   117

ACKNOWLEDGMENTS

Grateful acknowledgment is made to the following individuals and institutions that have contributed photographs and information to this book: the staff of the Walter P. Ruether Archives of Labor and Urban Affairs at Wayne State University—especially Mary Wallace for pictures from the *Detroit News* Collection, the still photographs from the Burton Historical Collection, Detroit Public Library, and especially David Lee Poremba for his professional assistance.

Grateful acknowledgment is also made to Dwayne Labakas, John Morrison of the Hockey Information Service, Jim Reed, John Butsicaris of the Lindell Bar, Budd Lynch, Lincoln Cavalieri, Ken Lindsay, Pam Janiec, Greg Innis, and Kathy Best for all she did over the years. If I missed anyone, *mea culpa*.

INTRODUCTION

Who could ever forget growing up in the Detroit area and fighting the winter cold and snow, walking into the Olympia Stadium from the parking lot on game night? Men wearing suits, ties, a hat from Henry the Hatter, and a long wool coat; women dressed up in their finest, with their hats and white dress gloves on; the ushers in their bright red coats and military style hats. The excitement of walking down the halls greeting other fans who had seats in the same section. It was a cross between enjoying good friends and a place to be seen. Remember running up the 101 steps to the balcony to stake out a standing room space as soon as the doors opened?

Remember sitting in your seat as the visiting Montreal Canadiens took the ice wearing their white jerseys with the CH crest on the front with their great leader Rocket Richard skating around the ice warming up? Then moments later, from the other bench, the crowd standing and a loud roar would come up as the Stanley Cup Champion Detroit Red Wings took the ice, and the building started to come alive.

The Production Line of Lindsay, Howe, and Abel; Terry Sawchuk in goal; Tony Leswick, Marty Pavelich, Glen Skov, Metro Prystai, Johnny Wilson, Jim Peters, Bill Dineen, Vic Stasiuk, Dutch Reibel; and the defensemen: Red Kelly, Marcel Pronovost, Benny Woit, Bob Goldham, Leo Reise, and Larry Zeidel, all ready to do battle. In those days they didn't wear helmets or name tags on their backs, but everyone knew all the players by name and number.

After the national anthem, Lefty Wilson and Tommy Ivan would go behind the bench and Wally Crossman would man the gate to the ice, Red Storey would be ready to drop the puck at center ice while linesmen Art Skov and Matt Pavelich stood by to call the offsides; the puck was dropped and it started—another great memory in the building we all called the Old Red Barn on the corner of Grand River and McGraw. This was the night of the week we waited for—Red Wings hockey at the Olympia.

For over a half-century the world's greatest hockey players played at the Olympia Stadium. But the Olympia was more then hockey, it was the number one entertainment venue in Detroit in its time. The greatest shows on earth came there to perform. The ice shows with Sonja Henie, circuses, the famed Lippazanner Horses from the Spanish Riding School in Vienna. Who could forget the wild nights when wrestling was the main attraction or championship fights? Remember the Olympics in the '30s or the Olympics of the '60s playing lacrosse? The Black Watch from England? The Globetrotters and the Pistons? The great concerts with star performers like Elvis, the Beatles, John Denver, Frank Sinatra, the Who, and many other rock groups on their way to the top. The Grinnell's piano concerts where hundreds of youngsters dressed in white paraded on to the floor to play the over 100 pianos together as proud parents and relatives watched.

In 1926 John Townsend and Wesson Seyburn returned from the Montreal meetings with a hockey franchise for the city under the name of the Detroit Winter Palace, Inc. At that time the new arena was to be built on Jefferson, east of Woodward. The site on Antoinette between Woodward and Cass as well as the Fairgrounds were also considered possibilities. But finally Grand River and McGraw won out.

By the time Townsend and the new group were ready to do business as the Detroit Hockey Club, Charles Hughes was president and Townsend was the vice president. It was then that the group enlisted many of the members of the Detroit Athletic Club to come on board. The list of stockholders in the new venture was basically the membership roster of the DAC. It was then that they hired theater architect C. Howard Crane—the same man who designed the Fox—to design the new stadium.

In 1933 James Norris took over the Olympia and the Detroit Hockey Club, and it remained in the Norris family until they closed in 1979. The final game was considered just another game. No special TV ceremonies like we have seen in the closings of the other original six arenas. We just said goodbye, walked out, and went home. The next game we went to the Joe Louis Arena. The only farewell was the Last Hurrah, a game played between the then current Wings and the Old Timers on February 21, 1980. It was only fitting that the Greatest Red Wing of them all, Gordie Howe, would score the last goal at the Olympia.

One
THE '20S

The first event held at the newly opened Olympia Stadium on Grand River and McGraw in Detroit was a rodeo. The International Rodeo ran from October 15–22, 1927. Tickets were available from the box office at the Olympia, Rayl's downtown, and from the offices of Macumber-Smith in the General Motors building. Ticket prices ranged from 50¢ to $2.00 each, plus tax for the two-a-day shows.

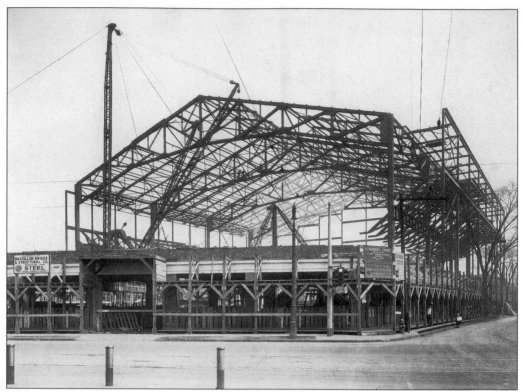

Looking at the corner of Grand River (front of building) and McGraw (right side of building), this view shows the early days of construction. The general contractor was Walbridge Aldinger Co. Frank C. Merlo and Co. did site excavation while Truscon Steel did the roof and Iron City Engineering installed the electrical system. Other contractors included United Cork Company, which insulated the floor and the plumbing, and Robert E. Purcell completed the heating.

This 4 by 9-inch ink blotter was an early advertisement for the Detroit Cougars and the opening of the Olympia. The first games were played across the Detroit River in Windsor, Ontario at the Border Cities Arena, now the Windsor Arena. The advertisement noted that opening of the Olympia was to be January 15, 1927.

The balcony, which was quite steep, was being completed before the walls were even finished. The steep slope allowed for great viewing of hockey games with little obstructions. There were 101 steps to reach the balcony and some people feared going up there because of the steep slope. In later years the standing room in the balcony became a favorite place to watch games because the ticket prices were cheap. When the doors opened, fans would run up the stairs to stake out their spaces to watch the games.

This photo, taken on August 30, 1927, showed that there were trees on the McGraw side of the building. When the building opened two months later the Detroit Street Railway added 125 new streetcars. Most of the new ivory-colored cars were put into service on the Grand River run. When the Olympia opened, it was the world's largest indoor skating rink.

With the floor in place and the miles of brine pipes installed beneath, the building was ready for painting and the installation of the seats. Another temporary platform would be added around the floor for more seats, the players' bench, and the boards—or dashers, as they were called then. Dreson Brick supplied the red exterior bricks on the Olympia.

Reginald Nobel came out of Collingwood, Ontario, to play for the Montreal Maroons in 1926. In 1927 he joined the Cougars (and Falcons—the name was changed in 1930) and spent five seasons in Detroit. A solid left winger, he was traded back to the Maroons in December 1932, for Johnny Gallagher. He was inducted into the Hockey Hall of Fame in 1962.

Art Ducan became the first playing manager of the Detroit Cougars. Ducan was born in Sault Ste. Marie, Ontario, on July 4, 1894. Prior to coming to Detroit, he played for Vancouver and the Calgary Tigers. After one season he went to Toronto where he played four seasons before retiring at the end of the 1931 season.

The 28-page, 1926-1927 Detroit Cougars guide is one of the oldest publications put out by the new Detroit Hockey Club of the National League. The first three pages give the list of officers, directors, and owners of the Cougars. There are 22 pages about the players with their photos and the last three pages are the 1926-27 schedule of games.

13

The cornerstone was laid in March 1927. The Detroit Free Press had run a photo of Detroit's mayor John W. Smith with a trowel laying Olympia's cornerstone. Attending the ceremony were many of the Detroit Athletic Club members who backed the new building and the National Hockey League's president, Frank Calder. Pictured, from left to right, are: (front row) Detroit Hockey Club president Charles Hughes, Calder, Mayor John Smith, unidentified, and Lawerence Fisher, a club director; (back row) Detroit vice president John Townsend, J.L.Woods, James E. Devoe, and L.J. Lepper—all directors of the Detroit Hockey Club.

When the building was being torn down in 1986, the corner stone was discovered. It had been covered for years and no one had checked the records to find out about it.

After one season, Art Duncan was let go and the club management went after Jack Adams to run the team. Adams had won the Stanley Cup in 1918 with the Toronto St. Pats and in 1927 with Ottawa and had just retired at the end of the 1927 season. Adams would go on to win seven more Stanley Cups with Detroit.

Detroit Hockey Club

1927 · GAMES · 1928

DETROIT COUGARS
NATIONAL HOCKEY LEAGUE

All Home Games Played at

OLYMPIA
GRAND RIVER at McGRAW AVENUE
DETROIT

SCHEDULE OF GAMES

At Home	Abroad
Ottawa, Tuesday, Nov. 22	Pittsburgh, Tuesday, Nov. 15
Canadiens, Sunday, Nov. 27	Boston, Saturday, Nov. 19
Chicago, Thursday, Dec. 1	Chicago, Saturday, Nov. 26
Rangers, Sunday, Dec. 4	Montreal, Saturday, Dec. 10
Americans, Thursday, Dec. 8	Canadiens, Tuesday, Dec. 13
Boston, Sunday, Dec. 11	Rangers, Thursday, Dec. 15
Pittsburgh, Sunday, Dec. 18	Toronto, Saturday, Dec. 17
Montreal, Thursday, Dec. 29	Americans, Tuesday, Dec. 27
Ottawa, Saturday, Dec. 31	Rangers, Tuesday, Jan. 3
Canadiens, Thursday, Jan. 5	Pittsburgh, Saturday, Jan. 7
Toronto, Thursday, Jan. 12	Chicago, Wednesday, Jan. 18
Rangers, Sunday, Jan. 15	Rangers, Thursday, Jan. 26
Boston, Sunday, Jan. 22	Toronto, Saturday, Feb. 4
Chicago, Sunday, Jan. 29	Boston, Tuesday, Feb. 7
Pittsburgh, Sunday, Feb. 12	Americans, Thursday, Feb. 9
Chicago, Sunday, Feb. 19	Montreal, Thursday, Feb. 16
Ottawa, Thursday, Feb. 23	Pittsburgh, Saturday, Mar. 3
Rangers, Sunday, Feb. 26	Boston, Tuesday, Mar. 13
Americans, Thursday, Mar. 1	Canadiens, Thursday, Mar. 15
Toronto, Tuesday, Mar. 6	Chicago, Saturday, Mar. 17
Montreal, Thursday, Mar. 8	
Ottawa, Saturday, Mar. 10	
Pittsburgh, Sunday, Mar. 18	
Boston, Saturday, Mar. 24	

Pictured is the schedule for the 1927-1928 Detroit Cougars. This was Adam's first year at the helm of the Cougars and the team finished fourth in the American Division with 19 wins, 19 losses, and 6 ties for 44 points—only 2 points out of a playoff birth. The New York Rangers won the Cup that season as coach Lester Patrick donned the pads when his goalie got hurt.

On October 26, 1927, the first boxing match was held for the elimination match for the heavyweight championship of the world between Johnny Risko and Tom Heeney. Over 15,000 people were in attendance as Heeney won the 10-round affair. One of the writers covering the fight was Damon Runyon of *Guys and Dolls* fame.

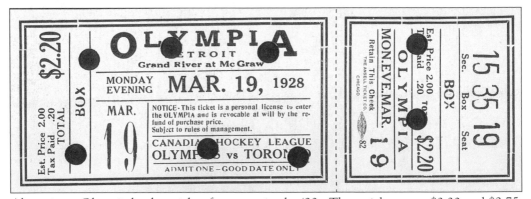

Above is an Olympia hockey ticket for games in the '20s. These tickets cost $3.30 and $2.75. In 1928 Henry Ford started his $5.00 a day for Ford workers.

Two
THE '30s

In 1933 the original owners of the Olympia defaulted on their mortgage payments to the United Guardian Trust Company, and Chicago industrialist James "Pop" Norris purchased the Olympia and the hockey club. He kept Jack Adams as general manager and changed the name of the team to the Red Wings. It was then that they went to the red and white uniforms. In the 1933-34 season the Wings were the league champions.

As people went out Grand River from downtown they would see the streetcar coming down the middle of the road, the Studebaker dealership, the Chinese hand laundry, and the Olympia.

The 1935-36 Red Wings captured their first Stanley Cup championship behind the goaltending of Normie Smith. On March 24, 1936, against the Montreal Maroons, the club played six overtime periods before Mud Bruneteau scored to give the Wings the win.

18

The front of the Olympia with its large marquee is pictured here. Parking was allowed in front of the building and on the Hooker side street.

A calisthenics exhibition by women of all nations was one of the many different events booked at the Olympia.

The Red Wings goalie makes a stop while the defense covers up. Smith wore the cap to shade his eyes from the glare of the lights. Goalies didn't wear masks until the 1950s.

The Wings won their second Stanley Cup in a row in the 1936-37 season, beating out the New York Rangers three games to two. Attendance for the final game at Detroit was 14,102.

Detroit Red Wings
1937 - 1938

Front Row: Doug Young, Hec Kilrea, Syd Howe, Larry Aurie, Carl Liscombe, Norm Smith.
Back Row: Mud Bruneteau, Marty Barry, Eddie Wares, Jack Adams (Manager), Ship's Captain,
Ebbie Goodfellow, Unknown, Pete Bessone, Alex Motter.

After winning their second Cup, the club traveled to England for a series of games against a Montreal Canadien-Maroons team. Some of the activities in England included bike races and royal receptions.

Jack Adams made Donnie Hughes the coach of the Detroit Olympics, which was a farm team for the Wings. Many of the players that season played for both clubs since they played all their home games at the Olympia. The Olympics were champions of their league in 1936-37.

In November 1938, Detroit hosted a political convention giving notice that they had the facilities to host other major events. In 1931 President Herbert Hoover addressed the American Legion convention being held at the Olympia Stadium.

The 1938-39 Red Wings finished fifth in the standings and beat out Montreal two games to one in the first round of the playoffs, but were knocked out by Toronto two games to one. Ebbie Goodfellow and Syd Howe were selected to play in the All-Star Game October 29, at the Montreal Forum and a youngster named Sid Abel was up to play 15 games for the Wings.

Three
THE '40S

On April 8, 1943, with the war on in Europe, the Wings beat Boston 2–0 to win their third Stanley Cup. Johnny Mowers got the shutout and Carl Liscombe was the leading scorer. After the playoffs many of the Wings were off to fight in the war. Note the "V" with three dots and a dash on the jersey sleeves—Morse code for "V", or victory.

On July 18, 1941, a new refrigeration plant was installed as 10 miles of piping were put in the floor. Brine was then lowered to a temperature of 10 degrees and fed into the pipes. Water was then sprayed on the cold floor. Layer after layer was sprayed on until the ice was three-quarters on an inch thick.

Detroit announcer Paul Williams presents Red Wing goalie Johnny Mowers the Vezina Trophy, for the goalie with the best goals against average during the 1942-43 regular season. Toronto's Turk Broda finished second.

The official team photo of the 1942-43 Stanley Cup Champions. It should be noted that team photos were shot during the season, not after the team won the cup. Thus some of the players that were on the cup never appeared in the team photos and some were in the photo but were traded or back in the minors.

Former Red Wing Bill Jennings, then with the Boston Bruins, took time to talk with long time usher Bill Opalewski, who was with the Olympia when they first opened. Note the collar and button down style of the ushers' uniform from the '40s.

One of the many recreation teams that played at the Olympia. Many evenings there were two games followed by public skating. This team was sponsored by Harry Suffrin Clothes store. The trainer, Percy Ferrel, worked around the Olympia well up to the 1960s.

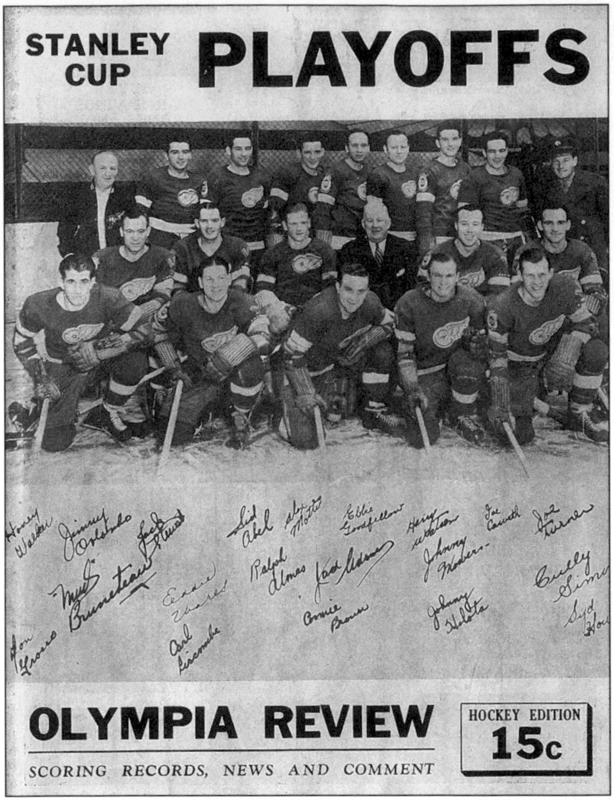
STANLEY CUP
PLAYOFFS
OLYMPIA REVIEW
HOCKEY EDITION
15c
SCORING RECORDS, NEWS AND COMMENT

The 1943 playoff's program from the Olympia Stadium. The player in the military uniform was Joe Turner, who was killed in World War Two. In all, 24 Red Wings had their careers interrupted to fight in World War Two, including future Hall-of-Famers Sid Abel, Harry Watson, and Jack Stewart.

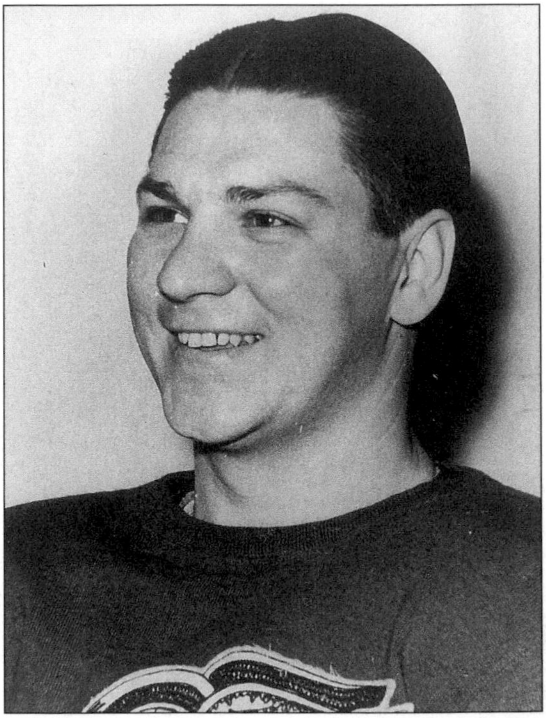

Carl Liscombe wore numbers 7, 10, 15, and 17 during his 9 seasons with the Red Wings. His first game was November 23, 1937, and his best season was 1943-44 when he scored 36 goals and 37 assists to finish fourth in league scoring. On November 15, 1942, Liscombe scored 3 goals and had 4 assists as the Wings walloped the Rangers 12 to 5.

For years Jacobs Brothers Sports Service ran the concessions department at the Olympia. These concession workers wore their military style, striped-collar uniforms. They sold everything from Frostbites to the programs.

In 1958 Bruce Norris hired Lincoln Cavalieri to join the Olympia Stadium Executive staff. One of the first jobs Cavalieri had was to buy out the Sports Service contract. It cost the Olympia $150,000 to get out of the contract, but it was well worth it as profits soared with the new company-run concession department.

Boxing was big in the 1940s at the Olympia. Joe Louis defended his title in a fight here in 1941. Ezzard Charles beat Jersey Joe Walcott. Toward the final years of Olympia, a young fighter by the name of Tommy Hearns started to make a name for himself.

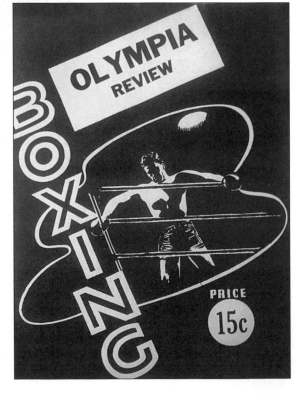

On Friday, February 25, 1944, Jake LaMotta, in front of a crowd of over 10,000 customers, defeated Ossie "Bulldog" Harris. This is the program from that fight at the Olympia that grossed $25,527.80. This was LaMotta's third win in a row over Harris.

Four

THE '50S

Bob Goldham congratulates Gordie Howe after a game. Goldham played on three Wings Cup teams plus one with the Leafs in the '40s. The all-star defenseman was known as a great shotblocker. After retirement he was an analyst for Hockey Night in Canada.

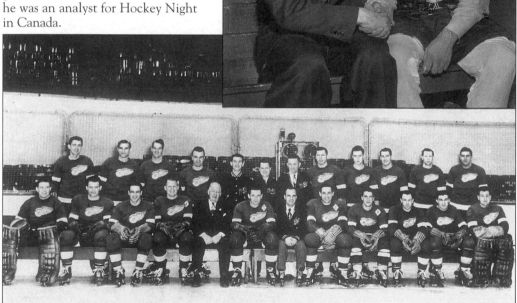

This team was part of the Wings' 1950s dynasty. With the Production Line in full swing, the New York Rangers met them in the finals. However, Madison Square Garden had the circus on, so New York moved into Maple Leaf Gardens for the finals. The series went seven games, as Pete Babando, assisted by George Gee, scored at 8:31 in the second overtime period on Charlie Rayner to clinch the cup. It was the first seventh game finals overtime goal in the history of the NHL.

The only way to make ice is to spray it on in layers. The ice is made to a .75-inch thickness for hockey games, and from time to time, has to be shaved to make it thinner.

Before the invention of the Zamboni or ice-cleaning machine, there was the shovel. Between periods a crew of six scrapers in their red wool sweaters would circle the ice pushing all the loose snow out the gates.

After the ice was cleaned, the water barrel was pulled around the ice leaving warm water on the ice to melt the top surface. When the ice froze up again in a few minutes, a new smooth surface was all ready for the game to continue.

The lines were painted on with a paintbrush and special paint. There were also special stencils for painting the circles, goal-crease lines, and the emblems.

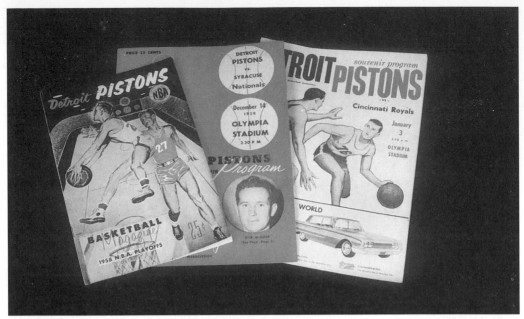

The Detroit Pistons, who had come up from Fort Wayne, played three seasons at the Olympia. Pictured are some of the programs sold for the games. The Pistons moved downtown when Cobo Hall was built.

For basketball games and other special events a special cover was put over the ice, with boards laid on the covers. Here an employee takes the boards back to the storage area after a game. Note the fence on top of the boards. It wasn't until later that a special glass was installed for hockey games.

From the catwalk high in the roof area of the building, the camera catches the maintenance crew at work assembling the boards for a basketball game. Many times, because of the Pistons and Wings schedules, the floor had to be torn down right after events at night.

The famous Bulova time clock that was located high above the ice surface. The penalty timekeeper ran the clock from ice level by the penalty box. The clock could be lowered to the floor level for repairs.

Chief usher Dick Smith has his crew out on the ice for a pregame briefing on October 8, 1953, before the start of the season. The Wings opened the season with a 4-1 win over the New York Rangers. Note the different styles of coats. The red hats with the Olympia in gold on them were used until the stadium closed.

Ice shows were always a big hit in Detroit. Pictured here is Andra McLaughlin who played hockey at Cheyenne High School. She was also an excellent figure skater and was asked to replace Sonja Henie in the Hollywood Ice Review when Henie started her own show. She is shown here appearing with the 1957 Ice Follies.

All-Star Red Kelly was one of the NHL's best defenseman during his career, and was the first player to win the Norris Trophy. It was at a dinner at a Detroit restaurant that he was introduced to Andra. In March 1955, they announced their engagement.

On February 27, 1957, this panoramic photo was taken at the southwest corner of Grand River. It shows the restaurant and car wash on Grand River, although neither are there today as they

were torn down for a parking lot. The marquee advertises the Red Wings-Montreal game and the Ice Follies for 1957.

Two of Olympia's workers take a break in the image above. Seated on the left is Red Tonkin, who ran the Olympia's ice operation and was in charge of building repairs during the 1950s. On the right is Scotty Watmuff, who worked in the Red Wings dressing room during the season.

In the summer, Grinell's Music of Detroit would sponsor the Michigan Annual Music Festival. The floor would have over 100 pianos set up and there would be two concerts with students from all over the Detroit area playing at once. This is the program from the 1950 performance.

General Manager Jack Adams poses for a photo showing his ace of diamonds—Gordie Howe. Howe scored 786 regular-season goals with the Red Wings and owned most of all the NHL awards. He wore numbers 17 and 9 during his great career and was nicknamed "Elbows and Mr. Hockey."

If it's springtime in Detroit, it must be playoff time. Here the Detroit fans lineup on Grand River with the line turning up Hooker Street. The Detroit Lions and the Chicago Bears were scheduled with the Globetrotters to play on Friday, March 29, 1963.

This *Detroit News* panoramic photo taken on February 27, 1957, from the southwest corner of Grand River and McGraw, looking east down the McGraw side of the Olympia Stadium. On

the northwest corner was a drug store that was torn down for parking. Eventually all the houses around the Olympia were bought up for much needed parking space.

Detroit Red Wings
Stanley Cup Champions 1951-1952

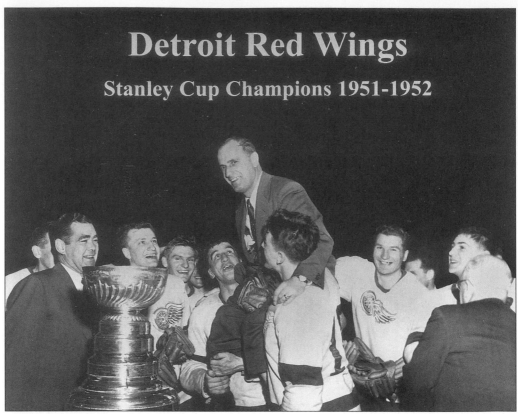

The Stanley Cup returned to Detroit in 1952 as the Detroit players hoisted coach Tom Ivan on their shoulders. Standing by the Cup is Jim Norris, Benny Woit, John Wilson, Ted Lindsay, Vic Stasiuk, and Terry Sawchuk. Jack Adams has his back to the camera.

The '52-Cup team was rated by many as the greatest hockey team ever. They won the league title by 22 points over Montreal and had the top two scorers in the NHL on their team. In the playoffs they won the Cup in eight straight games, with Terry Sawchuk posting four shutouts. Howe, Lindsay, Kelly, and Sawchuk made the All-Star team.

Tommy Ivan won his third and final Stanley Cup as coach with the Red Wings as Tony Leswick equaled Pete Babando's feat. In the seventh game in overtime and the score tied, Tony Leswick flipped the puck toward Montreal goaltender Gerry McNeil. Doug Harvey deflected the puck, passed McNeil, and Detroit had their sixth Stanley Cup

Looking down the ice from the end-zone boards, the rink is quiet and ready for the night's game.

Ross "Lefty" Wilson came up to the Wings as a trainer and spare goalie. Teams at that time used the trainer for practice and emergencies. If a goalie was hurt, it was the home team's responsibility to provide an emergency goaltender. Lefty played in three games as a sub with Detroit, Toronto, and Boston.

In 1955, with Tommy Ivan gone to the Black Hawks, Jimmy Skinner took over as coach of the Red Wings. Here he greets his team's stars, from left to right: Gordie Howe, Marcel Bonin, Glen Skov, Johnny Wilson, and Marty Pavelich. Note the underwear hanging on the wall. In those days players sat on a bench in the dressing room, which was quite small and cramped.

Jimmy Skinner was with the Wings organization well into the Joe Louis years. He coached the last Red Wing team to a Stanley Cup victory at the Olympia Stadium. He was appointed coach in July of 1954 after Tommy Ivan left. He coached for three and a half seasons and retired on January 2, 1958, due to health problems. Sid Abel assumed the coaching duties. In April of 1980, Skinner was hired to be the Red Wings general manager, a post he held until 1982.

On April 14, 1955, the Stanley Cup was rolled out to center ice and presented to Captain Ted Lindsay by the NHL's president Clarence Campbell. The first woman owner of a Cup team, Marguerite Norris, also accepted the trophy. From left to right are: Norris, Dineen, Campbell, Pronovost, Skinner, Delvecchio, Howe, and Sawchuk.

The 1954-55 Detroit Red Wings Stanley Cup Champions are pictured above. They beat out the Montreal Canadiens four games to three to win the Cup. The Canadiens were without Rocket Richard for the playoffs, who was suspended for hitting a linesman in a game. On March 17, the Canadiens forfeited the game to Detroit at the Forum, touching off the famous St. Patrick's Day Riot after one period of play.

On June 3, 1955, Jack Adams stunned the hockey world by trading super-star goalie Terry Sawchuk and three players to the Boston Bruins for five players. This allowed Glen Hall to take over the goaltending duties. Here he stops Boston's Bob Beckett. Al Arbour, wearing glasses, is behind Beckett. In July of 1957, Adams again shocked the hockey world by sending Hall and Ted Lindsay to the Black Hawks and trading John Bucyk to the Bruins to get Sawchuk back again.

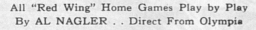
The famed Production Line of the Red Wings were a holy terror to opposing teams and goalies. The line consisted of Ted Lindsay at left wing, Sid Abel at center, and Gordie Howe at right wing. For three years in a row the whole line made the All-Star team. In the 1949-50 season they placed first, second, and third in scoring. Lindsay and Abel finished their playing careers with the Black Hawks while Howe retired from the Hartford Whalers in 1980.

One of the ads in the Red Wing programs featured radio station WKMH sending the play-by-play action of the Wings, with Al Nagler broadcasting. Note the games then started at 8:30 P.M.

The 6th Annual All-Star Game was held at the Olympia Stadium in October of 1952. In prior years the Cup champions would play the All-Stars at their arena. This year the team was a red and white jersied All-Star team. Pictured in the front row are: Bill Quakenbush, Elmer Lach, Terry Sawchuk, Marty Pavelich, Bill Mosienko, and Tony Leswick. Pictured standing are: coach Tommy Ivan, Ed Sanford, Gordie Howe, Doug Harvey, Reg Sinclair, Dave Creighton, Gus Mortson, Red Kelly, Leo Reise, Ted Lindsay, Bob Goldham, and president Clarence Campbell.

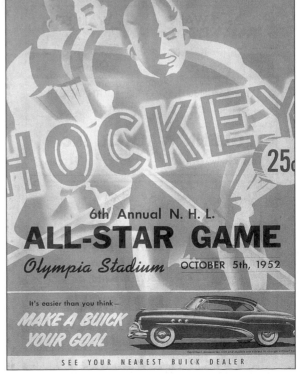

The October 5, 1952 All-Star Game program from Olympia cost just 25¢.

A view of the balcony from the end zone inside the Olympia. The press box, penalty box, and official timekeeper's area is on the left, with the team benches on the right. Prior to making separate penalty boxes with the off-ice officials in between, there was only one penalty box.

Both teams sat in it together with a big, burly usher in-between them to keep order. Note the new sound system and the scoreboard on the balcony.

With Ted Lindsay gone to Chicago, trainer Lefty Wilson holds up his old jersey with the familiar number 7. Four of the Red Wings who will be vying for the big 7 are, from left to right: Johnny Wilson, Tom McCarthy, Forbes Kennedy, and Guyle Fielder.

The player with two names, Enio Sclisizzi played parts of five seasons with the Red Wings, playing his first game on October 15, 1947. Public relations director Fred Huber was told people were having trouble pronouncing Enio's name so he changed it to Jim Enos. Thus, some photos refer to him as Jim Enos, others as Enio Sclisizzi. Jim was traded to Chicago on August 14, 1952.

Five
THE '60S AND '70S

Wrestling became big during the 1960s and '70s. The major headliner was bad boy Dick the Bruiser. In 1959 promoters Johnny Doyle and Jim Barnett drew 238,827 fans into the Olympia Stadium, taking in $544,957.00. The papers ran photos and stories of the Bruiser, usually ones like this with blood flowing on his head.

One of the biggest hooplas of the decade occurred on April 27, 1963, when suspended Detroit Lions star Alex Karras wrestled Dick the Bruiser. Karras is show here holding up one of his managers, Major Little. His other manager, Jim Butsicaris, stands behind the ropes.

Here the Bruiser puts an arm lock on Karras. The match lasted 11 minutes and 21 seconds, with the Bruiser winning. The crowd was a disappointing 8,000 to 10,000 fans. The Bruiser's real name was Dick Afflis, formally of the Green Bay Packers. Alex Karas wrestled under the title of Killer Karas.

54

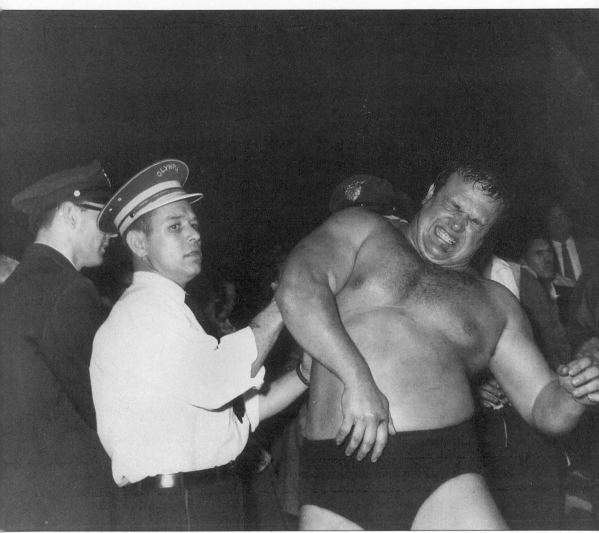

An Olympia usher tries to assist Detroit favorite Roul Ramero during his performance. Going into the crowds always excited the spectators, who clamored from front-row seats. *Wrestling Life* magazine in its June 1960 issue quoted promoter Johnny Doyle as saying, "Detroit has become of the world's greatest wrestling centers."

Twice during the 1960s the Beatles came to Detroit, in 1964 and 1966. The sold-out concerts had thousands on female teeny-boppers going wild. The above photo shows Paul McCartney and George Harrison singing. The noise and screaming was so loud during the concert that no one could hear them singing.

At a press conference behind the stage area, the Fab Four answered the same questions they had been asked countless times at other interviews. The big controversy at the time was their music and long hair. Above, Paul, George, John, and Ringo field questions.

One of the hottest tickets in Detroit on August 13, 1966, was for the 7:00 P.M. concert. This arena ticket cost $5.50 then. Wonder what it would cost at today's rates? To collectors in today's market, this ticket sells for over $100.

The Beatles didn't seem to faze the young boys, but the girls completely lost control as the Fab Four appeared on stage. Everyone seemed to have a camera, and standing by the stage looking into the audience it seemed like fireworks were exploding as flashcubes went off all over.

John Lennon, the famous leader of the band, thrills the crowds and especially the girls. His hairstyle and looks changed dramatically in the 1970s as the Beatles started a new art culture. He would be assassinated in later years.

Paul McCartney gives his sexy smile to the teeny-boppers while playing. Concessions manager Raoul Satori remembers cooking steaks in the alumni room for the Beatles to eat between shows, only to be told they just wanted American hamburgers.

Crowd control was a big problem at the shows. Both the ushers and police had to repel the girls from getting to the stage. Many of the fans were throwing the flashcubes from their little Kodak cameras, and photographers and ushers got pelted. One of my photos shows a large gym shoe landing on the stage.

Many fans sent flowers to the Olympia and the Whitney Hotel where they stayed. One enterprising individual wanted to buy the carpet from their room and cut it up into small squares for souvenirs.

One of the first Zambonis at the Olympia just had the name and Red Wing crest on the side. The Zamboni didn't start really being popular until the 1960s. At the 1960 Olympic Games held in Squaw Valley, California, the Zamboni was used for all the ice surfaces and offering the world an opportunity to see the future of ice maintenance.

The new Hercules 1900 boards being installed in summer of 1968. Tired of having to replace the wooden boards, Olympia's assistant general manager Lincoln Cavalieri had the new plastic boards installed. One-inch thick, the plastic was installed with adhesive and screws.

Lions football star John Gordie gives Detroit weatherman Sonny Eliot a kiss prior to a benefit game. Sonny, a popular TV star, was also signed to a contract with the Wings for $1.00. He appeared in several charity games, and in this one, he suited with the Wings to play their junior team. Gordie was there to play for the Lions against the local media stars in a pregame match.

Wearing a clear mask, these two young ladies help Sonny Eliot get ready to play goal. The big stick was little help, as some of the players wanted to see how close they could shoot at him before scoring. The masks was tried by several NHL goalies, but was discarded as it tended to fog up and cause the player to sweat more.

Coach and general manager Sid Abel checks out the Wings' dressing room prior to a game. Note how close the players were to each other when changing. The Tack skates were under the bench after being sharpened. In front of the number 7 jersey on the floor is an ashtray, as smoking in the dressing was not uncommon in those days.

On Junior Wings or recreation league game nights there was usually public skating afterwards. Wally Crossman, who had joined the Wings in the 1940s as a locker room assistant and skate sharpener, usually opened the Wings' skate room to sharpen skates and sell laces. Crossman was still with the Wings as the 2000 season began.

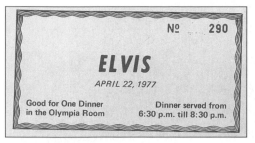

№ 290

ELVIS
APRIL 22, 1977

Good for One Dinner
in the Olympia Room

Dinner served from
6:30 p.m. till 8:30 p.m.

Some of the many different tickets for events at the Olympia. The 1951-52 season featured a roller derby. Wrestling tickets in 1961 cost $2.00, and the Monkees concert on July 29, 1967, cost $6.00 for arena seats. When Elvis played there on April 22, 1977, dinner was served in the Olympia Room.

The drugstore on the corner of Hooker and Grand River was popular with the Wings after practice. They could get a malt or milkshake after the 2-hour workout. Here Doug Barkley signs autographs while the owner looks on. Doug's milkshake is on the counter. The store also sold liquor and over the counter medicines.

This is the main concession stand on the left in front of the building that fans first saw when they came in from the Grand River entrance. To the right was the bar that opened before the doors did. Fans could get in the bar from Grand River and have a drink while waiting to get in, then go into the hallway by the door on the right.

Coach Sid Abel watches his team head out to the ice from the dressing room. Number 10 is Alex Delvecchio, number 7 is Norm Ullman, and number 9 is Gordie Howe. Note the signs on the wall by the doorway. The doorway on the right led to the lavatory and showers.

Prior to the new addition on the back of the Olympia in 1965, the press box was opposite the Wings' bench and hung under the balcony. It could be reached by walking to the last row of seats and then up another flight to the box. The TV cameras were out front as were the announcers. After the new addition was put on, a new press box was installed in the balcony and the old press box became private boxes.

Aerial photo of the area surrounding the Olympia Stadium during a matinee hockey game. On the far side of the stadium is the main parking lot. In the late 1950s and '60s, the Red Wings purchased all the homes in the area and made a huge parking lot extending back to the street behind the building and fenced it off. The tall building in the back is the Lee Plaza Hotel where some of the players stayed. To the left is Northwestern Field where many of the top local sandlot games were played.

Detroit Tigers star Willie Horton (left), played his high school ball at Northwestern Field as did many others such as Alex Johnson and Bill Freehan. Horton still remembers going over to watch the Wings practice. His favorite was Ted Lindsay, of whom he became friends with.

One of the many announcers' boxes displaying the different stations that broadcast the Wings games over the years. This is the visiting announcing crew using WXON TVs booth.

Two of the most famous announcers in the history of the Red Wings to do the play-by-play on radio station WJR. Hall-of-Famers Budd Lynch and Bruce Martyn were a very popular duo until Sid Abel came on to do the color with Martyn. Lynch, master storyteller and hockey historian, has held many jobs with the Wings including public relations director, goodwill ambassador, and public address announcer.

High up in the balcony press box, a youthful coach Scotty Bowman (second from right) of the Canadiens holds court with other hockey people. Pictured, from left to right, are: Montreal writer Red Fisher and Hockey Night in Canada's Dick Irvin, chatting with Wings assistant GM Jimmy Skinner. On the far right is the Canadiens' French announcer and former Montreal star, Gilles Tremblay.

From high up in the balcony came the live music. Seated at the organ is Art Quarto, who led the charge, entertained between periods, and played the national anthems. In the background is Father Lisee, who was the chaplain to many of the Red Wings and Olympia personnel.

Three of the Red Wing photographers pose in the press room next to the press box in the balcony. Pictured, from left to right, are: Robert Red Wimmer, who also worked for Hockey Pictorial; the late JD (Charlie Mac) McCarthy, who was better known for his sports postcard photography; and the Wings' long time photographer Jim Mackey.

King Clancy of the Maple Leafs used to tell everyone that they have Howe doing everything in Detroit, including selling peanuts between periods. Here Howe adds another job to his resume by assisting *Detroit News* photographer Scotty Kilpatrick.

Three of the Olympia's behind the scene personnel take a break at a Wings game. Pictured, from left to right, are: concession manager Raoul Satori, announcer Budd Lynch, and usher Bernie Opalewski, taking time to chat about the game. Opalewski joined his father as an usher at the Olympia and later went on to work at the new Joe Louis Arena in 1979 as a concession manager.

Two of Detroit's hockey writers for the *Detroit News* take time from having their free pregame meal in the balcony press box to get their picture taken. Seated is Jerry Green and standing is Vartan Kupelian. In the background is Wings' statistician Morrey Moorawnick.

The Red Wings' farm team coaching staff takes a break during training camp at Olympia. Pictured, from left to right, are: Vic Stasiuk, Wings GM; Coach Sid Abel; Cincinnati's Tony Leswick; and Hamilton Junior Wings' coach Eddie Bush.

Taking a break outside the Hooker Street front door are Red Wings Bill Gadsby (left) and Ed Litzenberger. Fans were invited to attend the 1961-62 training camp sessions by leaving a 50¢ donation to the United Foundation. Note the different teams that were in the Wings' training camp that season.

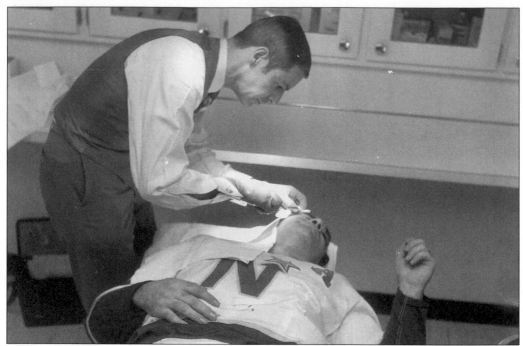

Cuts and bruises are nothing to hockey players. Here North Stars defenseman Leo Boivin lies on the examining table with all his equipment on in the first-aid room behind the Wings' bench (section 17) while team physician Dr. John Finley sews him up. Boivin was back on the ice within a few minutes.

Team dentist Dr. Florian Muske and team physician Dr. Milton Kosley watch as Dr. Finley works on sewing up a player. The three doctors worked closely with team trainers Lefty Wilson and Danny Olesevich keeping the players in top shape.

March 1969 finds assistant trainer and equipment manager Danny Olesevich sharpening skates and caring for all the Wings' equipment. Many times blades must be replaced and socks darned. In those days, if a jersey or sock had a hole in them they were sewn up and reused. Most of the players used CCM Tacks then.

Red Wings trainer Lefty Wilson was one of the first trainers to experiment with and design goalie masks. He made Terry Sawchuk's as well as others for local goaltenders. Here he is applying gauze to a player's face to make a mold for a mask. The goalie mask began to be accepted by players when Jacques Plante of Montreal wore one on November 1, 1959, in New York after being hit by an Andy Bathgate shot in the face.

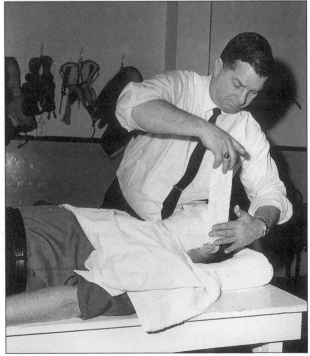

The voice of the Red Wings on WJR radio was Bruce Martyn and his sidekick and color commentator was Sid Abel. For many years they traveled with the team bringing the action of the game over the airwaves. A favorite expression Sid used to describe a play always began with, "Well Bruce there was a case of…" Note the boys are having a smoke in the booth while calling a game. Bruce and Budd Lynch were the cigar smokers while Sid smoked cigarettes.

Eventually the Zamboni accepted advertising as another way to make money. When advertising was first put on the boards, the TV stations protested and angled their cameras so as not to the show the free ads. Eventually the matter was resolved and advertising on the boards and all over the arena became a common practice for additional revenue for the teams.

Wings public relations director Ron Cantera presented the new members of the Red Wing Hall of Fame their awards. Pictured, from left to right, are: Ted Lindsay, Ebbie Goodfellow, Cantera, Doug Young, and Normie Smith. The Hall of Fame showcase was located near the front of the Olympia by the McGraw side of the building.

Two of Detroit's Stanley Cup goalies pay off golf wagers at a charity tournament. Norm Smith (left) was the first goalie to win a Stanley Cup for Detroit in 1936 and in 1937. Terry Sawchuk (right) won three Cups for the Red Wings in the 1950s and is considered to be the greatest goalie ever in hockey.

The Red Wings alumni, often called the Old Timers, were very instrumental in putting on charity events such as hockey games and golf outings. This photo shows the alumni and friends after a golf outing. The Detroit Red Wings alumni were a very big part of the activities in and around the Detroit area. The alumni club was started on November 1, 1959 when 13 former players met at Butcher's Inn at the Eastern Market to form the new organization.

Wings trainer Lefty Wilson gets together with former Wings public relations man Fred Huber. Fred was also a baseball umpire at Northwestern Field and worked with amateur hockey in Michigan.

The alumni had their own meeting room at the Olympia. It was located high on the lower level of the Grand River and McGraw corner (behind section 6). Members, from left to right, enjoying refreshments between periods are: Stu Evans, Rollie Roulston, George Gee, Nic Cinor, Norm Smith, and Red Doran.

Hockey was a family affair in Detroit. Here Jim Peters Sr. and Jimmy Peters Jr. get together before a Wings-Old Timers game. Both father and son played for the Red Wings. There were 20 families of fathers, sons, and brothers that played for Detroit.

This is the office of the Olympia Agencies, which was located in the rear of the building on the McGraw side. At one time it was the offices of the Wings public relations department as well. It was here that Gordie Howe had his office as a vice president and where he issued his famous Mushroom Speech.

High above the ice in the WKBD TV50 booth, Sid and Bruce are joined by Wings vice-president Lincoln Cavalieri while broadcasting the game. When the building addition was built in 1965 it added 1,800 more seats. At that time a long escalator was added in the back of the building to get people up to the balcony quicker.

During training camps assistant general manager Jim Skinner (left) and general manager Sid Abel often worked in the front concession stand to plan which players they wanted to keep and who was going where. Note the food prices: 30¢ for a red hot and 15¢ and 25¢ for soft drinks.

General Manager Sid Abel poses with his dog, given to him by owner Bruce Norris, who raised them. The dog was almost as big as the players. It was given to Sid to present to his son Gerry as a Christmas present. The dog, named Oliver, was a Newfoundland.

Down on the main floor by the visiting teams' dressing room was the main souvenir concession stand, run by Joe Gentile. He sold everything from the *Hockey News* and *Hockey Pictorial*, to the bobbing head dolls on the top for a dollar each. On the right are the JD McCarthy postcards of the players, media guides, lucky rabbits feet, Wings pins, and t-shirts. They didn't sell big-ticket items at that time such as jerseys and it was all cash, no credit cards. Anyone need a Wings hat?

To get to and from the ice, players had to walk down the hall and up the aisle. Here Gordie Howe and Billy Harris walk past the fans after the game. Eventually rails and a portable tunnel were installed to protect the players from the fans.

William Opalewski, second from right, was an usher when the Olympia first opened. Eventually his sons and other relatives joined him at the Olympia. He passed away while working at the Olympia and was buried with his usher's hat.

This was a very popular landmark in Detroit for people to see while driving from downtown out by Grand River. The glass windows were all bricked up but the big letters stood out for blocks. The restaurant and car wash on the building side of McGraw and Grand River were gone to make way for a parking lot and grocery store. In 1967 the Olympia was right in the middle of

the Detroit riots. Many of the local stores were looted, thus starting the exodus to the suburbs. The following year the Tigers won the World Series and the Red Wings finished last in the Eastern Division on the newly expanded 12-team National Hockey League.

This is the main front lobby facing the bar and display case. In the center of the floor was a large Red Wing crest. Again you can notice the big ash tray containers by the walls. In the glass display case by the bar is a model of one of the Norris freighters— the SS *Red Wing*. The door on the right led to the Grand River lobby and the ticket windows.

"The Great One," Wayne Gretzky, and the Edmonton Oilers made only one appearance at the Olympia. On November 7, 1979, the Wings won 5 to 3. This was the year that four WHA teams joined the NHL.

The Red Wings' Christmas parties were always a big event for the players and their families. Many of the players were away from home and this gave them a chance to enjoy the holidays together. Seated on Santa's lap was Garry Unger, with his fancy cowboy jacket on.

Several of the players and their wives watch Santa hand out gifts. Pictured, from left to right, are: Danny Olesevich, Poul Popiel, Danny Lawson, and Roy Edwards. Christmas Day games were very popular with the fans, but not the players. In 1971 the Wings played their last Christmas Day game and in 1972 played their last Christmas Eve game.

In a pregame ceremony Gordie Howe was honored for scoring his 700th goal. His former teammates, other members of the Production Line, Ted Lindsay and Sid Abel presented Howe with a floral arrangement made with red and white flowers showing the number 700. Howe scored number 700 on December 4, 1968, at Pittsburgh as Detroit won 7–2.

One of the most popular attractions to appear at the Olympia was the Globetrotters. One game on Friday, March 29, 1963, saw the Detroit Lions play the Chicago Bears as a pregame warm-up for the Globetrotters.

These are the tan seats in section four from row G to row P. Behind the seats is the standing room area. This section was by the corner of Grand River and McGraw. The Red Wings Alumni Room was by this section in back. During games the fans with standing room tickets would sneak down and sit on the steps next to the seats. This practice was common, except on sellout nights when the fire marshall would show up and have the ushers clear the isles. Section 4 was also the visitor's end for the games.

In 1970 Pete Stemkowski picked up this brand new Dodge Charger RT at the dealership and drove back to the Olympia to show it to his teammates. Checking out Stemmer's new wheels are, left to right: Bob Baun, Poul Popiel, Gary Unger, Ron Harris, and Pete and Matt Ravlich. Stemkowski and Unger were living in Dearborn then and were frequent visitors to the Moby Dick on Schaefer.

On Sunday September 8, 1974, popular stunt driver Evil Knievel was shown on closed circuit TV on the big screen at the Olympia. Seats were $10.00 each. Tickets were available at Sears, Hudson's, Grinnell's, and the Olympia.

Bill Gadsby was in his second season as coach when, after winning the first two games into the 1969-70 season, he was fired. The next home game, October 19 against St. Louis, the fans came out in support of Gadsby. To show their displeasure with owner Bruce Norris, they picketed in front of the Olympia before the game.

On March 16, 1977, Ted Lindsay was hired as general manager to replace Alex Delvecchio. His motto was "Aggressive hockey is back in town." A line of clothing was put out plus hockey pucks with the new slogan. The Wings responded to the new slogan and went from last place in 1976-77 to second in 1977-78.

If You Haven't Been Getting Very Much Action Lately, We've Got Just The Ticket To Help You Succeed!

The Red Wings started up their own junior team in 1959-60. Under the coaching of Jimmy Peters, the Junior Wings produced some top players. Here the team celebrates winning the title. Pictured, from left to right, are: #16 Bobby Thomas, Jimmy Joe Smith, Don Jaeger, Jocko Hancock, Jim Peters Jr., Jim Howland, Bob Libby, and Jerry Spinelli. Kneeling are Ned Runey and Pat Rupp.

Celebrating on the ice after winning the title are #20 Warren Hilly, #8 Dick Devine, Bob Libby, and captain Jimmy Joe Smith. Hilly went on to play at Michigan State, Libby played for the U.S. Army in Germany, and Smith went to the Winnipeg Monarchs.

Pictured above are the Junior Wings of 1959-60. In the first row, from left to right, are: Bob Libby, Nick Musat, GM Dan Distel, Jim Clement, coach Jim Peters, Roger Taylor, and Ron Bunarek. In the second row are: assistant trainer Jim Osborne, Jimmy Joe Smith, John LaPierre, Jim Howland, Bill Breault, Doug Roberts, Chuck Shottroff, Jerry Spinelli, Don Harris, Ned Runey, and trainer Percey Farrell. Missing are Dick Devine, Bernie Roach, Steve Landis, Clark McCaw, Dan Jaejar, Bob Thomas, and Jim Peters Jr.

JUNIOR Red Wings '60-'61

SOUVENIR HOCKEY MAGAZINE

BORDER CITIES
- LEAGUE -
JUNIOR "B" O.H.A.

CHATHAM
DETROIT
DRESDEN
LEAMINGTON
RIVERSIDE
WALLACEBURG
WINDSOR

OLYMPIA STADIUM
DETROIT
25¢

The 1960-61 Detroit Junior Wings' program, lists the other teams in the Border Cities League on the cover.

Newly appointed coach of the Memphis Red Wings Jim Peters talks to two of his new players: Jim Peters Jr. on the left and Doug Roberts on the right. Both players were products of the Detroit recreation league and the Junior Wings with Jim Sr. as their coach. Peters went to Hamilton to play Junior-A hockey while Roberts played for Michigan State. Both Roberts and Peters went on to NHL careers with the Red Wings. Jim Jr. is now the athletic director at Vermont Academy.

After the Junior Wings, the Olympia allowed many recreation teams to play there. One such team was the Stu Evans team. Former Red Wing and Montreal Maroons player Stu Evans, who owned several Mercury dealerships in the Detroit area, sponsored the club. Evans is seated fifth from the left in the front row. Standing on the end in the second row is Joe Burt, who was the trainer and worked at the Olympia.

These posters showing the Howe boys and their dad displayed the Olympia Agency schedule. The team also played some of their home games at the Windsor Arena.

93

This was one of the most exciting Junior Teams to play in Detroit. It was a family effort as many of the players' families got involved including the Howes, with the Olympia Agency sponsoring the team. The Red Wings were mired in last place under Ned Harkness' leadership and the crowds were down. However, Detroit took the junior team to its heart and really supported them. There were sellouts for their games.

The team lineup was: (front row) in light slacks assistant coach Ernie Asadoorian, Steve Miskiewicz, Kevin O'Rear, Ron Serafini, Jim Lanzi, Marty Howe, Bill Ciraulo, Jim McCarthy, and head coach, Carl Lindstrom; (second row) Doug Ross, Scott Jesse, George Case, Gary Kardos, John Asadoorian, Pat Donnelly, Tom Esper, and assistant coach Dick Malcolmson; (third row) Bill Fraser, Frank Werner, Bob Dobek, Doug Reed, Mark Howe, and Dave Fulton.

Hall-of-Fame curator Lefty Reed was in town to catch a Red Wings game and visited the Alumni Room. Pictured, from left to right, are: Hall-of-Famers Sid Abel, Alex Delvecchio, , alumni president Bill Gadsby, Larry Cain, Lefty Reed, and Black Jack Stewart.

At the start of the 1966-67 season the Wings had some awesome firepower on the front line. Pictured, from left to right, are: Dean Prentice, 242 goals; Andy Bathgate, 306 goals; Gordie Howe, 624 goals; Norm Ullman, 268 goals; and Alex Delvecchio, 311 goals. Even with all that firepower, the Wings finished fifth and were out of the playoffs.

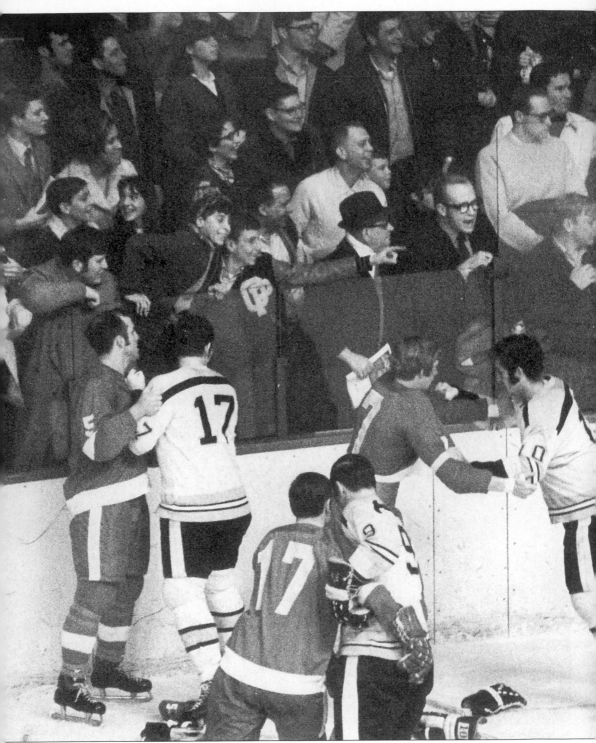

Invitation to a dance. The Boston Bruins, the Red Wings, and all the fans get into the action on this fight. That was the closeness the Olympia offered. The glass wasn't that high either as the fans could stand or lean over it. On the right, #16 Ron Harris and Nick Libett in front of

Harris (see skate #14) go at it with John McKenzie, who Libett has down. Others Wings include #5 Carl Brewer, #7 Garry Unger, and #17 Wayne Connelly. The Bruins players are #9 John Buyck, #17 Fred Standfield, and #10 Rick Smith.

Hockey has been a family affair for years. Dennis Hextall holding his #22 Red Wings jersey displays it for his father. Dennis' father, Bryan Hextall Sr., on the left, was a player for the New York Rangers during the 1940s, won the 1942 scoring title, and was inducted into the Hall of Fame in 1969. Dennis' brother Bryan also played for the Wings, and his nephew Ron played goal for the Flyers. The other three-generation NHL families were the Patricks and Abels.

The media stars were another team that played for charity. Here they pose for their team photo as they get ready to play the Detroit Lions prior to the Junior Olympic-Red Wing game in 1971. Pictured, from left to right, are: (front row) Kelly Burke (ch. 7), Bob Hynes (ch. 7), Ted Pearse (ch. 4), Jim McKay (Windsor Star), Ron Cantera (Wings PR), Dick Purtian (WXYZ), and Tom Kelly (WJBK Ch.2); (back row) Ray Lane (TV 2), Roger Pineau, Louie Schuck (WXYZ), Jim Davis (WXYZ), Bill Coombe, Bob Fofch, Mike Kenny (WXYZ TV 7), and unidentified.

Visiting team usher Fred Jahn welcomes Atlanta Flames coach Bernie "Boom Boom" Geoffrion in for a game. They are standing by the visiting team's locker room door located on the Hooker side of the building behind section 13.

The first Zamboni used in a NHL arena was in the Chicago Stadium for Sonja Henie's ice show. Frank Zamboni, the inventor, built the first model over a jeep. He drove it from California to Chicago on a trailer.

TV sportscaster Dave Diles interviews members of the Red Wings Old Timers down by the ice about their upcoming game at the Olympia against the Red Wings. Pictured, from left to right, are: Diles, Ebbie Goodfellow, Red Doran, Ted Lindsay, George Gee, and Carl Liscombe.

On October 14, 1964, the Wings purchased the rights to Ted Lindsay from Chicago, allowing him to make a comeback at age 39 after being retired for 7 years. He responded with 14 goals, helping the Wings to capture the league championship. Here he and former Black Hawks teammate Pierre Pilote watch the play.

Three well-known people around Olympia were *Detroit Free Press* hockey writer Jack Berry, maintenance and concessions worker Jesse Thomas, and Wings player Pete Stemkowski.

In 1970, the Wings hired Harkness to replace Sid Abel as coach. With Harkness aboard things were in a constant turmoil. On January 6, 1971, GM Sid Abel resigned and on January 8, Harkness was appointed GM. Doug Barkley was then appointed coach. On November 7, 1973, Alex Delvecchio was named coach. On February 6, 1973, Harkness resigned and on March 16, 1973, Delvecchio became the general manager. Meanwhile players were coming and going all the time, and during this era the Wings did not make the playoffs.

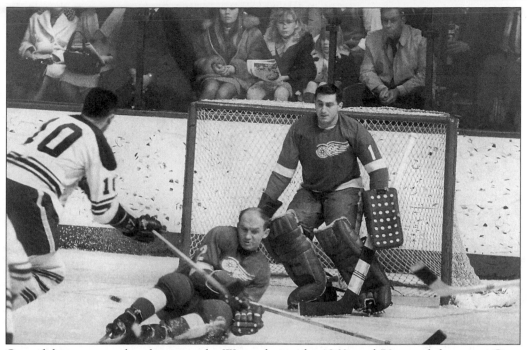

One of the most popular players on the Wings during the 1960s and 70s was defenseman Gary Bergman. Better known as Bergie, he was not afraid to get in the thick of battle as shown here. Going down to block Toronto's George Armstrong's shot much like 1950s Wings star Bob Goldham used to do. The Wings goalie without a mask is Roy Edwards. The last goalie not wear a mask was Andy Brown.

Bartenders and concession workers were a very important part of the Olympia. Up in the Alumni Room, Eddie Sophiea ran the bar and food trays operations.

These are the doors to the bar by the main Grand River entrance. The ship in the case by the window was the *SS Red Wing*, which was owned by the Norris family. The bar was decorated with large Red Wing photos on the wall.

Introduction of the former heroes of the Red Wings at an Old Timers game. Pictured, from left to right, are: Ted Lindsay, Jack Stewart, Johnny Mowers, Mud Bruneteau, Carl Liscombe, Syd Howe, Norm Smith, Ebbie Goodfellow, Bucko McDonald, Doug Young, Herbie Lewis, and unidentified.

Montreal Canadiens coach Scotty Bowman greets Mrs. Helen Adams, as they introduce the new book on the life of her late husband, Jack Adams, entitled *If They Played Hockey In Heaven*. Standing behind is the author, Phil Loranger.

Some of the many hockey publications put out and sold at the Olympia over the years. Top left is the 1966-67 yearbook featuring Gordie Howe, Roger Crozier, and Alex Delvecchio on the cover. Top center demonstrates the style of Wings programs in the 1960s. Top right was the 1930s fold out eight-page program called the *Puck*. Lower right is the late 1950s style program that was a smaller size. The 50th anniversary edition of the press guide featured the photos of the Norris family. Bottom center was the Red Wings-Montreal Old Timers program, which featured a reversed photo on the cover. Lower left was the 1950 playoffs program with Jack Adams on the cover.

The Mahovlich brothers, Frank and Peter, played two seasons with the Wings together, 1967-8 and 1968-9. While playing on a line with Frank and Alex Delvecchio, Gordie Howe had his only 100-point season with the Wings during the 1968-69 season. Frank was traded to the Canadiens on January 13, 1969, for Mickey Redmond, Guy Charron, and Billy Collins. Later brother Peter was sent to Montreal on June 6, 1969, with Bart Crashley for Garry Monahan and Doug Piper. While with Montreal, the brothers played on the 1970-71 Stanley Cup together.

Members of the 1943 Stanley Cup team get together at a Wings Old Timers meeting in the Alumni Room. Pictured, from left to right, are: Carl Liscombe, Joe Carveth, Don "the Count" Grosso, and Sid Abel, the team captain.

At a dinner dance to honor the 1936 and 1937 seasons, the former players got together to reminisce about the old days. Standing, left to right, are: Mud Bruneteau (who scored the longest goal ever in Stanley Cup history in the sixth overtime period), goalie Norm Smith, Syd Howe, and Ebbie Goodfellow. Seated are Bucko McDonald and captain Doug Young.

The first Monday of the month during hockey season was reserved for alumni meetings. Members seated, left to right, are: Art Bogue, Don Grosso, Larry Cain, and John Walters. Members standing are: Joe Klukay, Nelson Debenedet, Joe Carveth, Carl Liscombe, Sid Abel, Jim Peters, and Bill Gadsby.

Former Red Wing goalie Norm Smith presents the 1973-74 Stu Evans Trophy for most sportsmanlike on the Wings to Red Berenson.

An aerial view of the Olympia at an afternoon matinee with a packed house. The view is from behind the stadium looking west on McGraw. Notice all the cars that were parked around the building and across the street. In the early 1950s there were a lot of homes on the right side of the building (Hooker side), but the Wings needed the space, so they bought up and tore down all the old homes, making the area into a large parking lot. Many people can still remember parking on a side street in the area and having youngsters come up to them and asking, "Watch your car for a quarter or fifty cents mister." Watch it to do what?

Get together for a presentation prior to a game. Pictured kneeling, from left to right, are: Ted Lindsay, Gordie Howe, Gerry Abel, and Snapper Norris. Pictured standing are: Budd Lynch, Sid Abel, Carl Levin, Jimmy Skinner, King Clancy of the Maple Leafs, and Tommy Ivan of the Black Hawks.

No wonder we have trouble with games when the officials have problems putting on their uniforms. In the front is Budd Lynch followed by Doug Barkley. This photo was titled "One eye, One arm."

The Detroit Red Wings Old Timers posed for their pregame photo on the Olympia ice. Pictured, from left to right, are: (front row) Lefty Wilson, Gordie Haidy, Marty Pavelich, Jim Peters, Leo Reise, Joe Carveth, Doug Young, and Don Grosso; (back row) Joe Burt, Nic Cinor,

Joe Klukay, Gordie Howe, Hal Jackson, George Gee, Red Doran, Sid Abel, Bill Quackenbush, Carl Liscombe, Norm Smith, Ted Lindsay, Ebbie Goodfellow, Glen Skov, and Bob Goldham.

On March 12, 1972, Gordie Howe had his jersey and #9 retired. A host of dignitaries were on hand for the afternoon game against the Black Hawks. The highlight of the presentation was a visit from the Vice President of the United States Spiro Agnew. To Agnew's left is Tommy Ivan, Howe's former coach. On his right are Gordie and Colleen Howe, son Mark Howe, and daughter Cathy.

After retiring, Howe joined the alumni team. Here he jokes with retired Windsor Bulldogs' star Bobby Brown prior to a game.

General manager Sid Abel's biggest blockbuster trade occurred on March 3, 1968, when he dealt Floyd Smith, Paul Henderson, and Norm Ullman to the Toronto Maple Leafs for four players. Pictured, from left to right, are: Carl Brewer, Bobby Baun (acquired from the Oakland Seals on May 27, 1968), Garry Unger, Pete Stemkowski, and the Big M, Frank Mahovlich.

During the 1965 playoffs Abel assigned Bryan Watson to shadow Bobby Hull. He did such a great job that the Wings knocked off the Hawks four games to two. Hull was so frustrated by Watson that he called him "buggy" in the press, inspiring the nickname Bugsy.

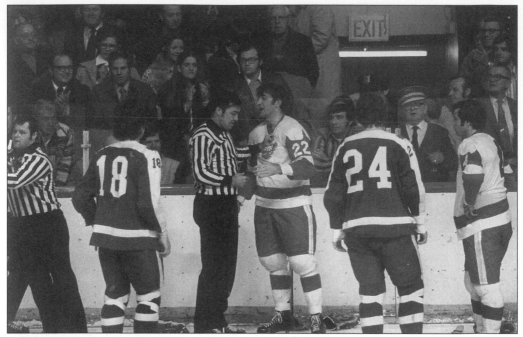

Linesman Matt Pavelich holds off #22 Bill Collins during a Leafs-Wings fight. Pavelich and Art Skov both had brothers playing for the Wings in the 1950s. When they would go into Montreal, Art Skov and Matt Pavelich would be the officials while their brothers Glen Skov and Marty Pavelich were playing for the Wings. Talk about stacking the deck.

On May 6, 1977, Red Wings general manager Ted Lindsay, in conjunction with Junior Wings general manager Tom Wilson, announced the hiring of Johnny Rea as the head coach of the Junior Wings. In 1969, as coach of the St. Clair Saints, Rea coached them to the National Junior "B" championship. The Junior Wings competed in the Great Lakes Junior Hockey Association.

Six

DECEMBER '79
AND THE '80S

Who could ever forget the wax-coated cups at the Olympia?
Very sturdy, they sold over a million cups of beer a season.
After finishing their drink, some fans would put them on the
floor upside down and smash them with their foot causing a
loud bang to echo down the corridors that sounded like a gun
going off.

Members of the old guard meet at the new Joe Louis Arena on December 27, 1979, for opening
night. Six members who had spent a good portion of their lives working at the Olympia Stadium
were on hand for the game against the St. Louis Blues. Pictured, from left to right, are: Corporate
legal counsel Robert Cavalleri, vice president Lincoln Cavalleri, assistant secretary Patrick Lannan,
buildings operation manager Jack Austin, Alex Delvecchio, and Mickey Redmond, TV announcer.

Red Wings magazine

Dan Labraaten
one of a series of souvenir covers

Quebec Nordique's goalie Goran Hogosta looks away with a "why me?" expression as the Red Wings Greg Joly just tied the score at 4-4. Danny Bolduc #19 and Paul Woods congratulate him as the Wings were down 4 to 0 in the second period. Greg Joly scored the last goal at 18:35 of the last period assisted by Paul Woods.

This was the program for the last NHL game played at the Olympia Stadium against the Quebec Nordiques on December 15, 1979. Danny Labraaten was featured on the cover. Bobby Kromm was the Red Wings coach and Jacques Demers coached the Nordiques. Attendance was 15,609.

The marquee shows the final NHL game and date, December 15 at 7:30 P.M., Red Wings vs. Quebec. It was also the JB Robinson Diamond Night promotional giveaway night. I wonder how many people kept their giveaway from the final game?

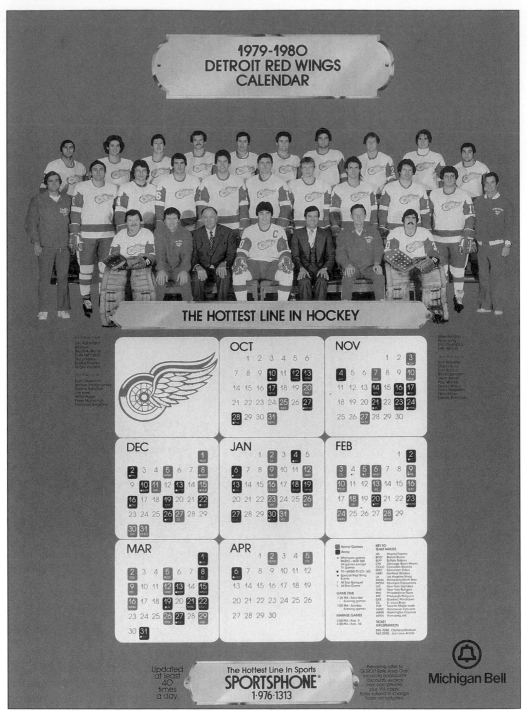

This is the large poster that was given out at a game as a promotional item for Sportsphone. Sportsphone was a number people could call to get the latest scores of events, and was updated frequently. The photo shows the last team to play at the Olympia Stadium and the first team to play at the new Joe Louis Arena.

On February 21, 1980, the Red Wing Old Timers assembled a team from their past heroes to play a game called "The Last Hurrah." That night they played the current Red Wings. Pictured, from left to right, are: (front row) Tom Shaw, Mickey Redmond, Ed Giacomin, Billy Dea, Joe Carveth, Jim Peters, Red Kelly, Tommy Ivan, Marty Pavelich, Bill Quackenbush, Rollie Roulston, Dr. C.L.Boone, Roger Crozier, and Pit Martin (back row) Art Skov, Art Bogue, Frank Mahovlich, Norm Ullman, Bill Collins, Jack Stewart, John Wilson, Bill Gadsby, Bryan Watson, Gerry Abel, Alex Delvecchio, Ted Lindsay, Larry Johnston, Neil Armstrong, Gordie Howe, Marcel Pronovost, Gary Bergman, Sid Abel, Nelson Debenedect, Carl Larson, and Matt Pavelich.

This was the last media guide put out by the Red Wings from the Olympia Stadium. The editor was Kathy Best, who ran the Red Wings public relations department. The media always turned to Kathy for help, and she always came through, being the ultimate professional in her job.

Loaded on the semi trailer are the letters that spelled Olympia from the Hooker side of the building. The "O" from the McGraw side was stolen one night when some fans climbed up on the roof during the Fourth of July fireworks downtown, disconnected the letter from the side, and carried it down and out of the building.

An entrepreneur spirit hit the local workers working at the demolition sight and some employees were selling seats on Grand River in front of the Hooker street parking lot. A few motorists stopped by and took a seat home for their recreation room.

Driving up Grand River from downtown, drivers saw the building half torn down. The rear was down, as the company worked their way to the front.

In a cloud of dust the front of one of Detroit's most famous landmarks was starting to make its last stand. The wrecking cranes worked from inside the building tearing down the walls. The building was built so well that implosion couldn't be used.

Prior to the demolition of the Olympia, former Red Wings public relations director Elliott Trumbull planned a last get together for all the old gang for a final tour of the building. Pictured, from left to right, are: Tommy Lynch, who was the Wings locker room attendant; Budd Lynch; Neil Shine, publisher of the *Free Press*; and Johnny Wilson.

Everyone showed up for the final tour of the building, which had been vacant for over six years. Pictured, from left to right, are: Budd Lynch, Ruth Hoffman, Gordie Howe, Jim Peters, Art Skov, Alex Delvecchio, Marcel Pronovost, and Billy Dea.

124

Out on the floor where the ice once was, Billy Dea, Art Skov, John Wilson, and Raoul Satori make the final pilgrimage around the building before the final hammer comes down.

In the Red Wings dressing room with the walls' paint peeling, former Red Wings stars Marcel Pronovost, left, and Gordie Howe, center, talk with former public relations director Elliott Trumbull about where they sat for many years while playing for the Wings. With all the power out in the building, flashlights lit everything.

Today the corner of McGraw and Grand River houses a new structure for the Michigan National Guard Armory. Tanks and military vehicles now are parked where once hockey fans watched the Red Wings play.

For the final get-together and unveiling of the new plaque, three of the old guard were in attendance. Seated is Kathy Best, and standing is Mike Giadarno and Terry Murphy.

These were the people who spent a good part of their lives working and playing at the Olympia Stadium. They came to say goodbye and to honor the new plaque that would be placed in the main entrance to the Armory.

Five of the players, whose playing days went back to the 1930s, were in attendance to help unveil the plaque that would commemorate the site of the Olympia Stadium. Pictured, from left to right, are: Alex Delvecchio, Johnny Wilson, Carl Liscombe, Stu Evans, and Bill Gadsby.

Alex Delvecchio and Stu Evans remove the cover from the plaque honoring the sight where the Olympia stood since 1926. Evans played from 1930 to 1939, while Delvecchio's playing career was from 1950 to 1974.

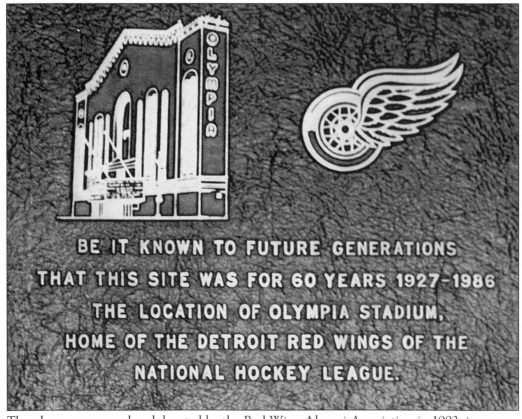

BE IT KNOWN TO FUTURE GENERATIONS
THAT THIS SITE WAS FOR 60 YEARS 1927-1986
THE LOCATION OF OLYMPIA STADIUM,
HOME OF THE DETROIT RED WINGS OF THE
NATIONAL HOCKEY LEAGUE.

The plaque, sponsored and donated by the Red Wing Alumni Association in 1993, is now on display in the lobby of the Armory on Grand River and McGraw.